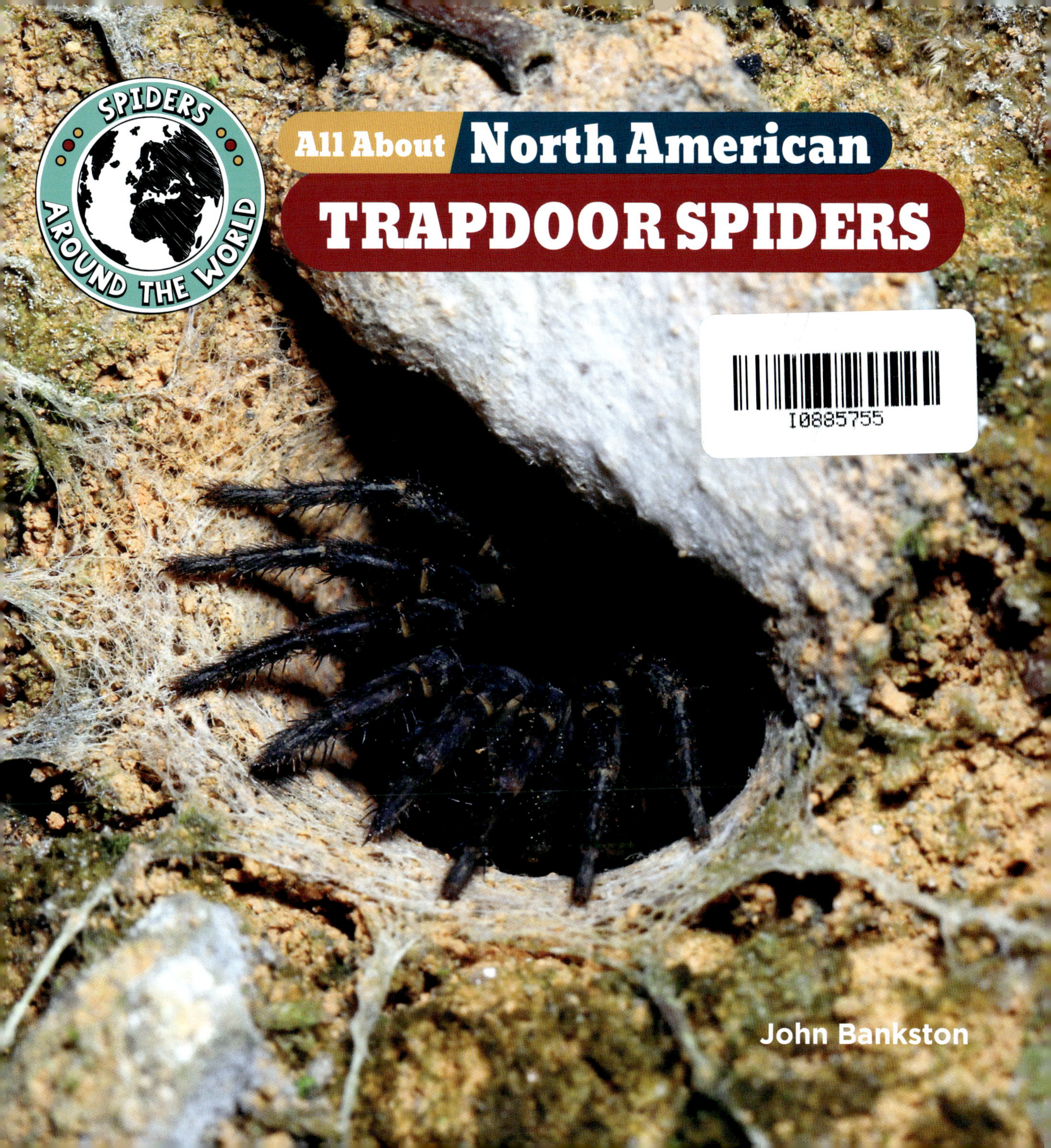

SPIDERS AROUND THE WORLD

All About North American TRAPDOOR SPIDERS

John Bankston

Mitchell Lane
PUBLISHERS
2001 SW 31st Avenue
Hallandale, FL 33009
www.mitchelllanepub.com

Little Mitchie

First Edition, 2025.

Author: John Bankston
Designer: Ed Morgan
Editor: Morgan Brody

Little Mitchie is an imprint of Mitchell Lane Publishers.

Title: All About North American Trapdoor Spiders
Description: Hallandale, FL : Mitchell Lane Publishers, [2025]

Series: Spiders Around the World: North America
Library bound ISBN: 978-1-68020-937-2
eBook ISBN: 978-1-68020-940-2
Paperback ISBN: 979-8-89260-164-1

Photo credits: Shutterstock

Contents

The cricket does not see a thing. It jumps beside a patch of dirt and leaves. The trapdoor spider waits below. Hairs on its leg warn it when the insect is near. Then it strikes!

The trapdoor spider shoots out of its hole. It wraps around the cricket like a fist. The bug is pulled below ground. The spider bites with its fangs. Now it can eat.

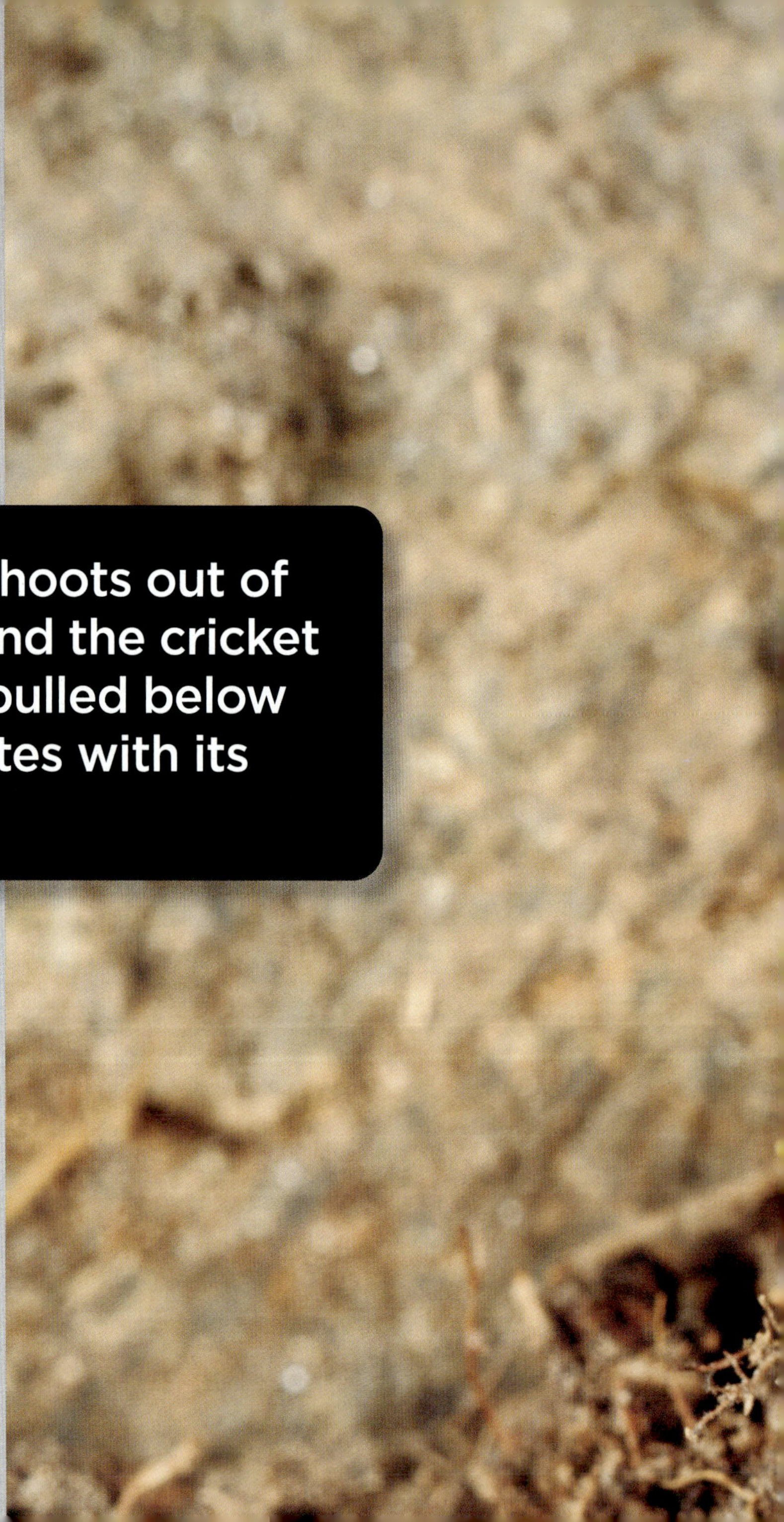

Trapdoor spiders live up to their name. They spin silk that covers their home's walls. Then they use silk to make a trapdoor. It's the shape of a penny. Dirt and leaves are pushed onto it. It's very hard to see. The spider raises the "door" like a lid.

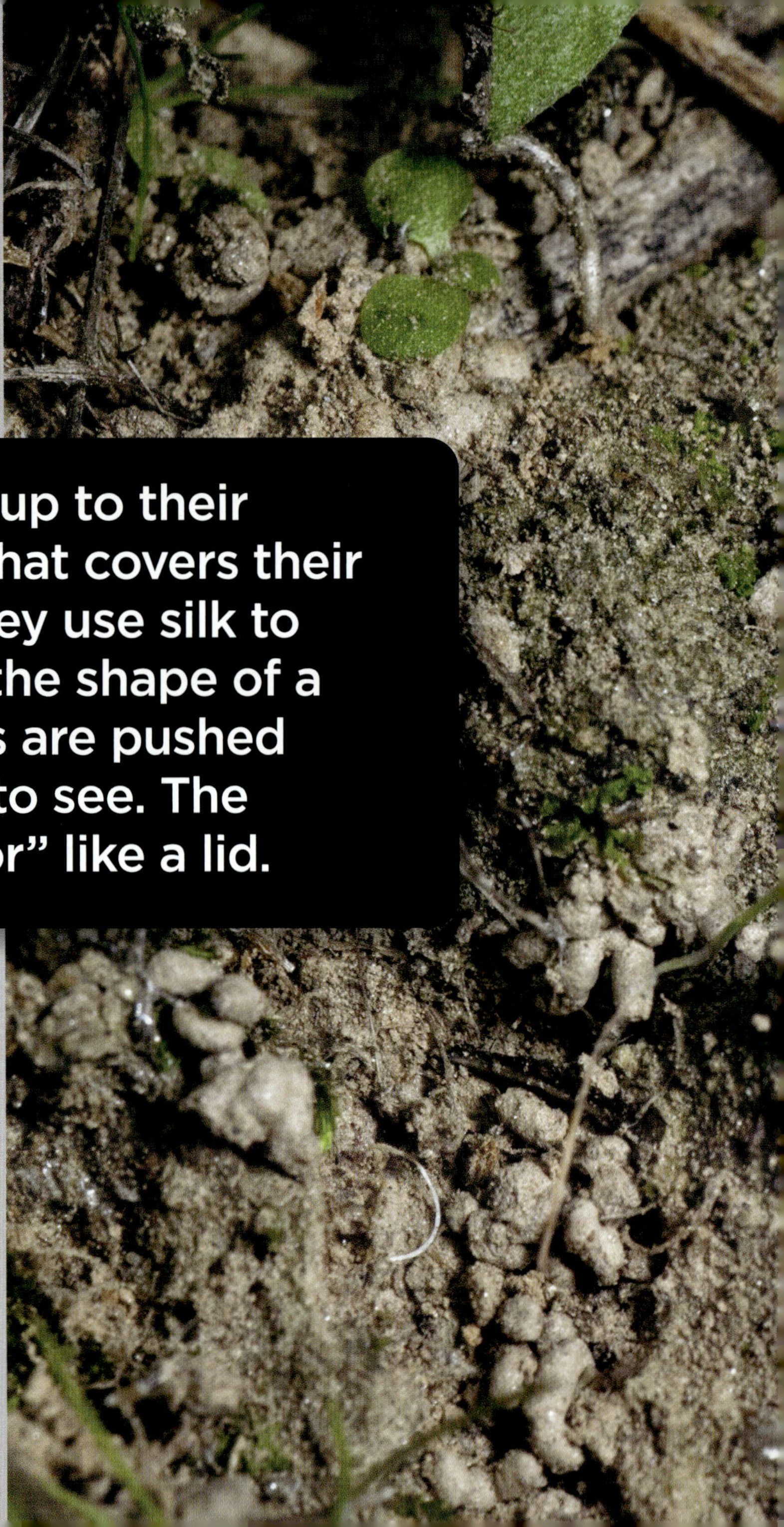

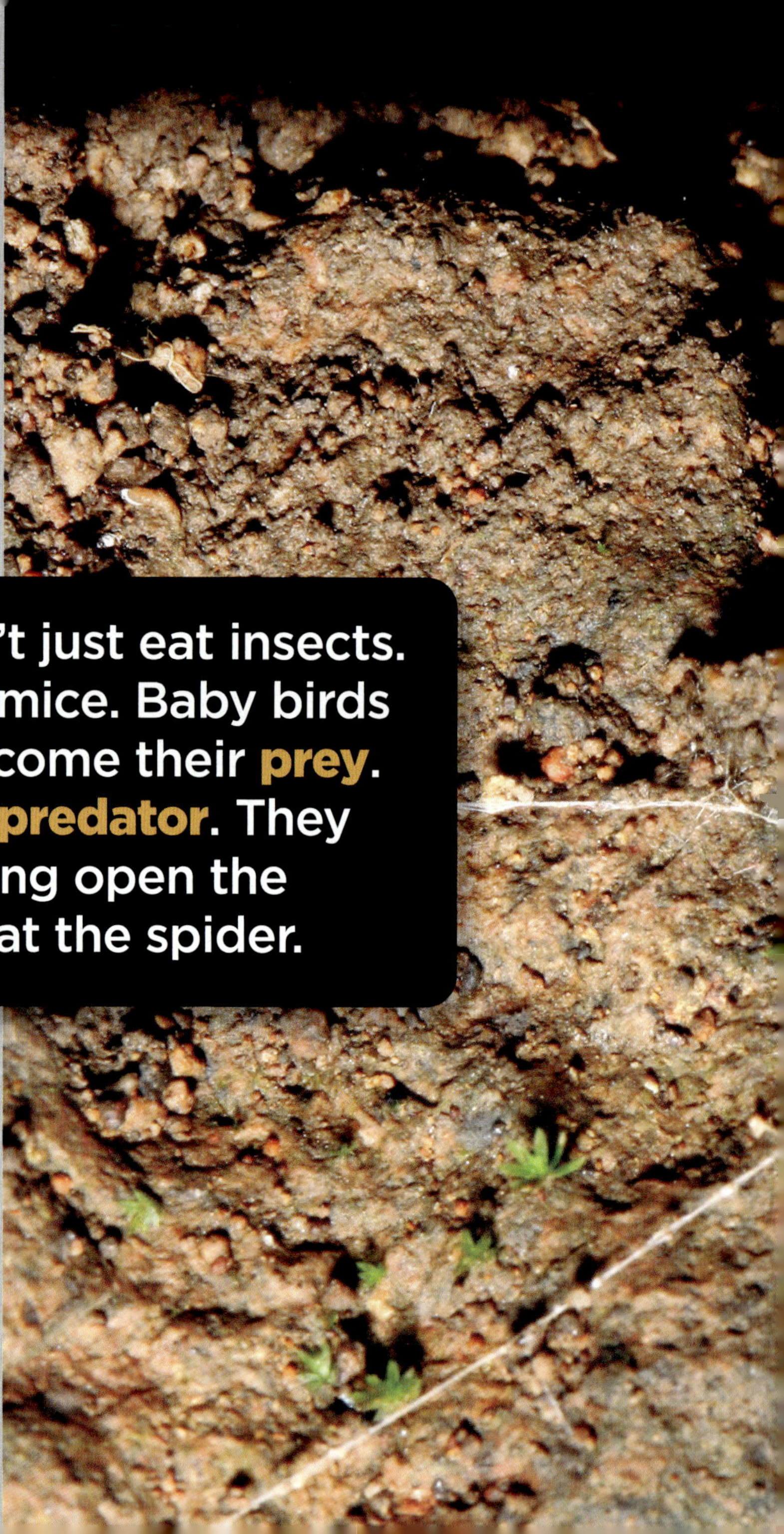

Trapdoor spiders don't just eat insects. They enjoy frogs and mice. Baby birds or snakes can also become their **prey**. Wasps are their main **predator**. They are very good at ripping open the trapdoor. Then they eat the spider.

Females kill males after **mating**. Males run away to stay alive. Female trapdoor spiders lay 200 eggs. **Spiderlings** live at home for months. Mother trapdoor spiders keep their babies safe.

Adult females do not leave their home. Spiderlings use their silk to make a kite. Then they fly away from home.

Trapdoor spiders are longer than your big finger. They like warm places. They keep to the ground. Their **burrows** can be found near trees or streams.

Trapdoor spiders are **nocturnal**. They only hunt at night. They wait for their prey to come to them.

It is very hard to find a trapdoor spider. Don't be afraid if you see one. They'd rather eat a bug than bug you.

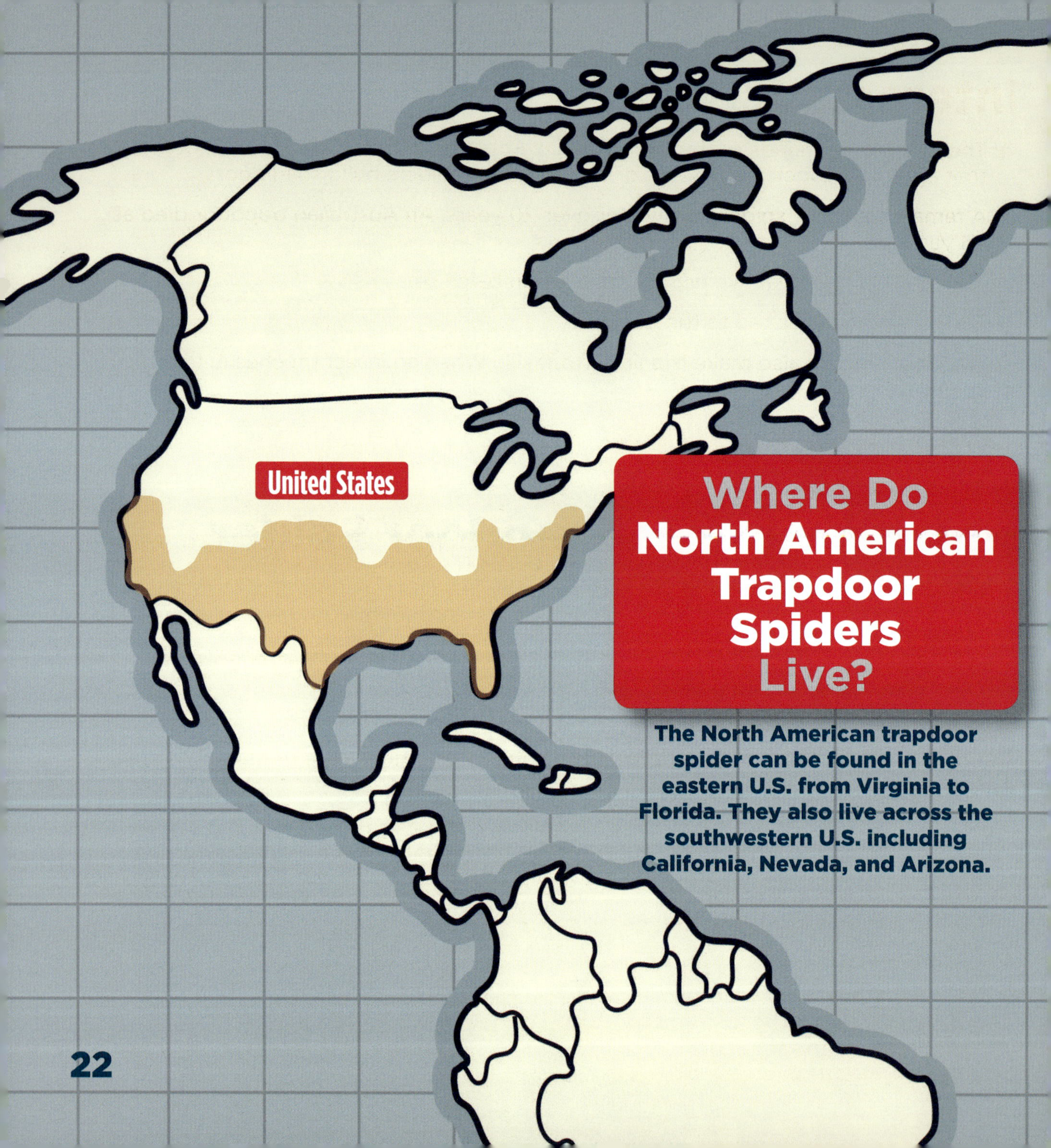

Where Do **North American Trapdoor Spiders** Live?

The North American trapdoor spider can be found in the eastern U.S. from Virginia to Florida. They also live across the southwestern U.S. including California, Nevada, and Arizona.

Interesting Facts

- The U.S. has two kinds of trapdoor spiders. Folding trapdoor spiders build doors that are folded open or closed. Cork-lid trapdoor spiders build solid doors.
- A female trapdoor spider can live for over 20 years. An Australian trapdoor died at 43 years old.
- Trapdoor spiders that live near streams often catch small fish.
- They are closely related to the tarantula.
- Trapdoor spiders also make trip lines from silk. When an insect touches it, the spider springs.

Parts of a North American Trapdoor Spider

Spiders are called **arachnids**. They have an exoskeleton on the outside of their body.

Abdomen
This spider has a very thick body. The **abdomen** and the **thorax** are almost the same size. The end of the abdomen fits tightly against the end of its hole.

Eyes
Trapdoor spiders have eight eyes. Two of the eyes are in the middle of its head. Three eyes are on the right, three eyes on the left.

Legs
Very thick legs are covered with hairs that sense **vibrations**. This alerts them to prey.

Mouth
The North American trapdoor owns a very strong jaw. Its sharp fangs stab like small knives.

Glossary

abdomen (ab-DOE-men)
Place where the stomach is located

arachnids (a-rack-NIDS)
An eight-legged creature without antenna

burrow (bur-ROE)
Hole dug by a spider

mating (MATE-ing)
When male and females of the same species come together to create offspring

nocturnal (noc-TURN-al)
Something that is most active at night

predator (pred-a-TOR)
Animal that hunts and eats other animals for food

prey (pray)
Animal hunted by another for food

spiderlings (spider-er-LING)
A baby spider

thorax (thor-ax)
The middle part of the body

vibrations (vie-brae-SHUNS)
What happens when something moves back and forth very quickly

Further Reading

Archer, Claire. *Trapdoor Spiders*. Minneapolis, MN: Abdo Kids, 2021.

All Things Spiders For Kids: Filled With Plenty of Facts, Photos, and Fun to Learn all About Spiders. Berlin, Germany: Admore Publishing, 2022.

On the Internet

Discover some interesting facts about the North American Trapdoor spider from A-to-Z Animals:
https://a-z-animals.com/animals/trapdoor-spider/

Learn all about the North American Trapdoor spider on Animal Corner:
https://animalcorner.org/animals/trapdoor-spider/

The Insider shows how trapdoor spiders Trapdoor Spiders Are Masters Of Surprise:
https://www.youtube.com/watch?v=ZH10-Jps47U

Index